And You,
BLESSED HEALER

And You, BLESSED HEALER

Boyd Warren
CHUBBS

BREAKWATER

BREAKWATER
100 Water Street
P.O. Box 2188
St. John's, NF
A1C 6E6

The Publisher gratefully acknowledges the financial assistance of the Canada Council which has helped make this publication possible.

The author acknowledges with true gratitude the support of the Newfoundland and Labrador Arts Council.

Several of the poems found within have appeared in TickleAce.

Cover painting and images by Boyd Warren Chubbs.

Author photograph by Justin Hall.

Canadian Cataloguing in Publication Data

Chubbs, Boyd Warren, 1995-

    And you, blessed healer

    (Newfoundland Poetry Series)

    ISBN 1-55081-118-5

I. Title. II. Series.

PS8555.H8A76 1996   C811'.54   C96-950240-0
PR9199.3.C4985A66 1996

Copyright © 1996 Boyd Warren Chubbs

ALL RIGHTS RESERVED. No part of this work covered by the copyright hereon may be reproduced or used in any form or by any means—graphic, electronic or mechanical—without the prior written permission of the publisher. Any request for photocopying, recording, taping or information storage retrieval systems of any part of this book shall be directed in writing to the Canadian Reprography Collective, 379 Adelaide Street West, Suite M1, Toronto, Ontario M5V 1S5. This applies to classroom usage as well.

For my Mother,
Una
and my Father,
Gordon Victor
1914·1995
My teachers and friends...
Sea people

PREFACE
Revelationist Poetry

Naturally, Boyd Warren Chubbs commences this book, his fourth collection of poetry in seven years, with a cunning pun: "The Passage" refers to not only a channel or a journey, but also the topography of reading. Of course, he signals his poetics, a weatherly 'elements of style', by superimposing one of Occidental civilization's catalysts, namely, the Hebrew and Greek scriptures, with the merciless and unutterably holy geography of Newfoundland and Labrador:

> Jesus died on his way to Calvert—couldn't hear
> his name against the wind, against the glitter in
> it; couldn't lift his head to see the massive form
> tumbling to claim him.... The Bible seems pale,
> somehow, against it all. Any book is poor against
> it. Even the true books need more nerve.

For Chubbs, the natural power of Calvert conquers the formal power of the faith initiated at Calvary. More importantly, though, this classic, post-colonial rewrite demands a poetry of "nerve," a verse as sternly majestic as the territory it names. It also engenders a transplanted religion, a Celtic-Pagan-Xian blend, a Canadian Mormonism.

Chubbs toils assiduously to adorn his world with an unapologetically watercoloured language, eschewing both the bleach of Atwoodish minimalism and the smirching Rorshachs of Mouré postmodernism. Starting with his astonishing debut, *Lines from the Migrant Coast* (1989), Chubbs champions a preternatural, melodic lyricism:

> I must gather one flower
> It will lean against another
> then another
> until they'll lean across the field[.]

In *And You, Blessed Healer*, he wins an even more unabashedly beautiful poetic line:

> Snow holds the stains
> until the rains take them, bend
> seasons to hide the day, draining the tough evidence,
> the earth opening and closing
> losing the wounds and cries living made
> We turn from the ribbed sounds
> sliding the blinds down—sip tea and memory[.]

Tinges of the great bardic poets—Blake, Yeats and Thomas—shade Chubb's work, but he assimilates their achievements, reconstituting them as comrade visionaries of fierce and magic coasts. Chubbs reaches deep into English—its history, its makers, and its rhetorics—to patriate all its potent resources.

It is no accident that Chubbs should hail from Canada's most spurned province. Unsung, unnoticed, but also uncompromised Chubbs and other Newfoundland and Labrador writers and artists have created English Canada's most lively and original (i.e. unamerican) culture over the past decade or so. Mary Dalton, Gerry Squires, Bill MacGillivray, Michael Crummey, and John Steffler, to name only a few, have forged a unique and stunningly rich canon of letters, art and film. Their works affirm the superior intellectuality of the Screech-oiled symposia conducted in the public salons of St. John's and Happy Valley/Goose Bay.

Scorning the Aesthetic *Junta*'s blather that poetry is dying, Chubbs fronts a new generation of Anglo-Canadian poets who compose in a 'Revelationist' mode, that is to say, with Soul (in the African-American sense), who seek to touch their audience. For poets like Chubbs, Steven Heighton and Dionne Brand, the duty of the poet is to sing to a congregation of readers (or auditors), to garb the nakedness of formal and informal poetic structures with the plenitude of passionate, open song. They recognize that poets must still translate emotion and intellect into hard, edible English.

For Chubbs, each poem must spark a great leap forward in the collective consciousness of his perceivers , whether they live in St. John's, Saint John or Lac St-Jean. His inner music is New World biblical prophecy:

> Down in the harbour town
> old chapters are whipped by words
> new language doing their backs. Whips
> to split wood those sounds and they split
> the old lies like birch with frost[.]

This voice knows that every poem must be cast as The Word—communal gospel passed from hand to hand like manna. This voice knows that the beloved poet declaims ag0ainst moneyed noise, the dirge of democracy.

An accomplished guitarist, calligrapher and artist—a late Renaissance man living Blake's dream—Chubbs has fostered, through pain and intuition, through wine and longing, a tongue and a faith that honour the wellsprings of song. Loving the "beauties past memory and the world tumbling," loving "the treaty of language making and unmaking," loving "large talk of immortality," his work wroughts a fresh dawn for poetry. Salute this *bon vivant*, credit this *compleat* bard, adore this mapper of a *home*. Praise him, not with "paper fire," but with the adoration of your lips shaping his words.

George Elliott Clarke
Durham, North Carolina
Nisan 1996

The Passage

Bring me a string for my old bow. There's a raw, solemn song needing flight, needing some passage to the center, he said, or was it myself I heard, a self-witness to a sight and sound crucifying us this year; most years. Jesus died on his way to Calvert—couldn't hear his name against the wind, against the glitter in it; couldn't lift his head to see the massive form tumbling to claim him. That's the edge of the weather this year—most years. Can't open the eyes against it. Got to find some place to wait. The Bible seems pale, somehow, against it all. Any book is poor against it. Even the true books need more nerve.

An ocean of make-and-breaks stutter somewhere in the memory cells and the steady curl of water from the stems fold into a wake going forever, through and beyond the stone cathedrals of Bay de Verde and other parishes, to Okak and past.

There are deaths this year apart from any explanation. Bodies in strange places, faces of new masks down our homeland's hallways—the long stretch on these walls of mute testimonials.

And how can the chaos be explored by any form, for form is order. How can this chaos, the speech about it, be achieved through order. How can the purpled form beneath the rafter be shown by ordered forms and the sound condemning walls of kitchens be heard and believed through poor and losing grammar.

This is a tough year for love. Beloved Healer, the clothes I wore over hills, through passageways and unmarked rooms don't warm me anymore. This is strange and new weather, a strange and crude way of breathing has pushed into our lungs; through our rattled skeletons. Suggestions for exiles and other jurisdictions busy pages not our own. Ignorant recipes to scatter us. A soul could curl into stone by some windows where young and old swallow the weather in.

Where I stumble and burn I sing the anthems sustaining me: sun, moon, berries, cliffs, water, light, dark, moss, heat, frost, storm, calm, accordions, song. They appear and reappear regular as love, in a passage of resonance against it all, teaching me the healing of home.

How Can I Travel That Country

I don't know water
I don't know how it can be
How can I see through
to its roots, to its plantation beneath the wharf
And how can I drift my hand,
a vagrant fin through its nothingness
And how can it shoulder ships
and swimmers going home
Stones where they chatter;
trout where they scatter and stray;
buckles, brooches and buckets;
spars, sprockets and sunken lights that blink
when the winds shift and the bay is ink
and a flight of jumpers
breaking from the foam like prayers,
how can they be in that nothingness,
that long-spoken liquid tongue
a story-storm wept, sung, danced, shivered about
If I could see how it makes itself
how it creates its long slumber of moves
and how its bold soul
rears at awkward and failing times
against the rocks and mind,
could I enter through by love and know its name
down in the anchor and bone garden
and rise with its groove
and plummet through with the fierce mane Druids knew

But how can I travel that country
that place of liquid nationhood
where father and brothers once stood
and cried and sang in their need
from the fading, flat-seamed wood

From Here Clear to Shea Heights

From here clear to Shea Heights
flights of gulls, ravens and metal, roaring arrows
split the sky and farther east,
upon the striking water,
a lone freighter tips west to the harbour
and again the sea is left to itself,
few keels rubbing through anymore

Beneath the East and Startled Moon

Beneath the east and startled moon
I lower with the faultlines
stonelines dropping in prayer through the Widow's Walk
to the bare loam of the stirred water
Father, brother, sister, mother
the woodcut against the unspoken east,
the burn of the wintered hours,
turn against the space holding speech in
Corpse or brute-fish surging,
all held away in the luminous, tidal tanks,
calling, calling against the fin of time and memory
Across this fist of rock and bone;
across this fist of wind and stone
watchers, waiters, pagan and god-like
strike the long bell, ears cocked for an echo
and eyes bulge across
for some sign through terrible and strangled time

The stacked and slanted layers;
the folded, molded layers of age and fire,
loom against winter where the east moon strays
and water drinks the light thin

In the Landwash

There's a sweat upon the rocks
Though they have the crust,
the stirred, ribbed crust of millennia,
they sweat and shift like strangers
Their fire, their blazing, spitting fire
from the massive regions of their centers,
has settled in a flat sweat—a dampened stove
in the center of a mad season

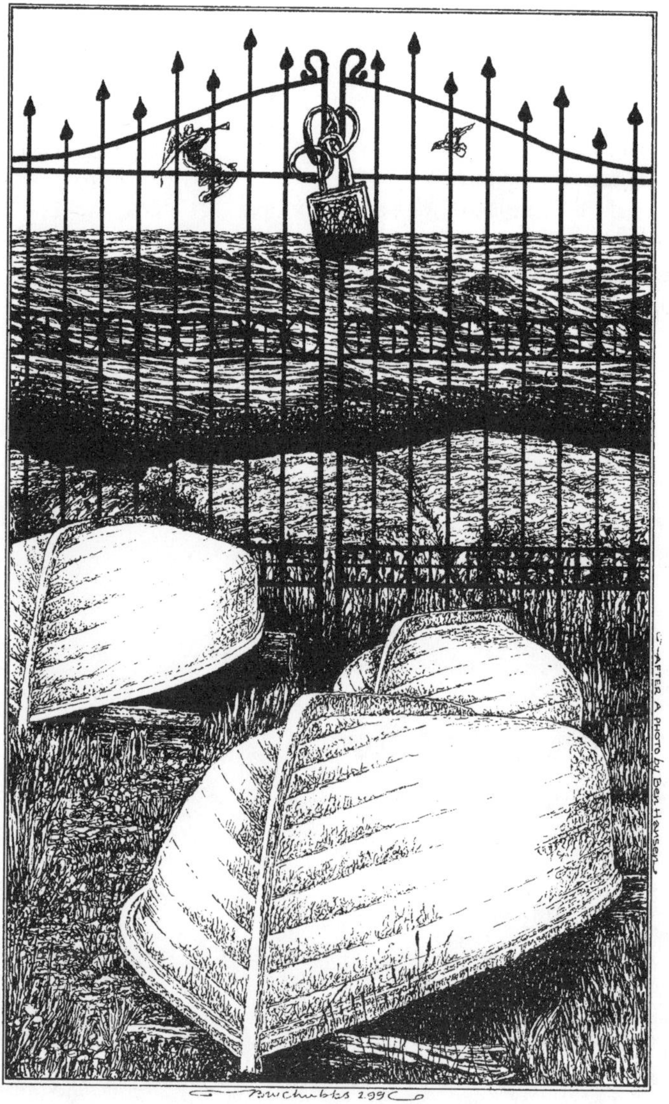
AFTER A PHOTO by Ben Hansen

Father, There's a Fog

There it is again and again
the all-over fog, desperate lover;
stayer and player of mad times
with mariners and pickers—
surreal anesthetic across wave and berry top;
cinematic memory from time and heart
I call it the warm wind's frost
dropping to thick sleep with the dog,
twisting boats and bog

In the Village
a Rumour is Many Things

It's a prejudice, a thick swath of it
dying good seasons. It's a massive boulder
down the hill through the sheds
into the low, bright kitchen
where children clown by candle-light

Feel its gravity; its damp-bone vortex
pull stumps and ruin boats
It's a matter of sleeps;
it's a matter of hollows before time, too,
is circled and swallowed

Words for William

Lean away from love, William
That part made my friend blind
and mumbled him, leaving him across Port de Grave
in the Baccalieu fog stumbled, mumbled and poorly-brave

Tonight, lean away from love
that circling light and laser
It could make death live, but turn
turn from her lie, the nerve crucified
like loss and fever. Sea and time
play a warm lop, a true chapter
where you stagger past the strangely-bred
Follow those saviour elements to your boat
and sleep upon the thick planks. Lean
toward the holy rhythms there for the grieving
the liquid breathing of whales and mermaids
beauties past memory and the world tumbling

We are old too, William
as old as the distance this world has dragged you
has dragged the province-souls
And one tear down your rough face
holds all trace, the deep carbon of every quake and plan
True lullabyes of sea and time for your heart
and they'll warm a passage through
the strange creek of blood
and the rattling stones, too
will find a clear way past Baccalieu

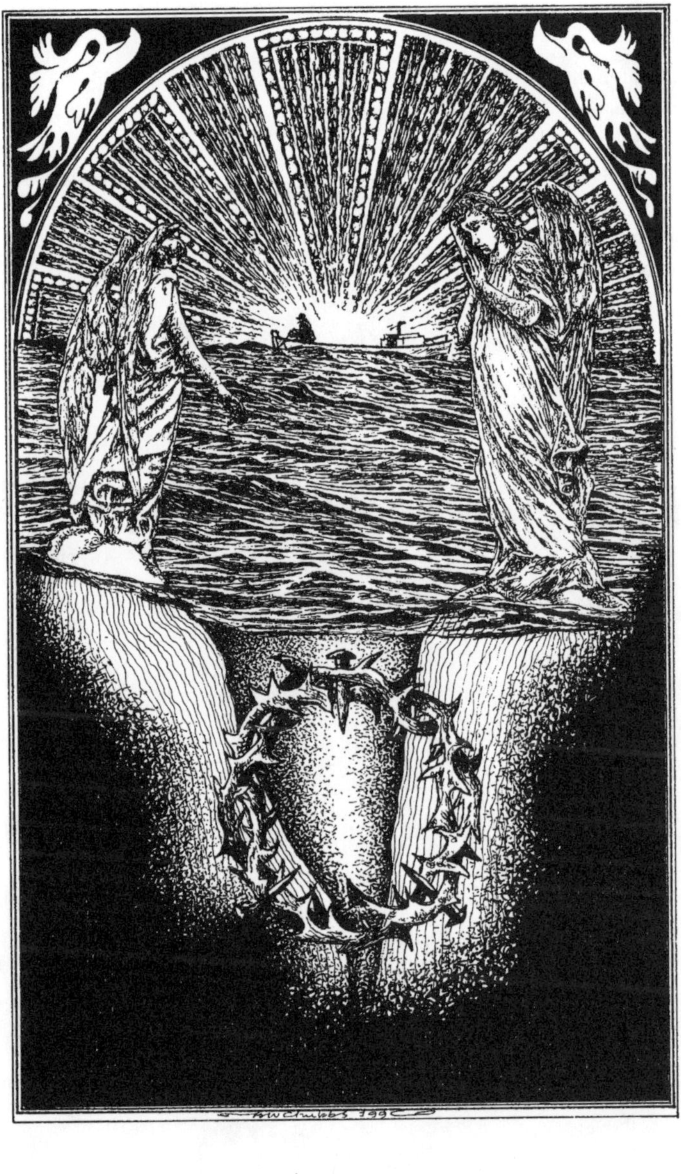

It Was a Mad Place

Through the hemlock, over the rock
past the poor boards where Emily said
ministers light Satan's candles
and make his bed,
children, dogs and elders fled
singing bread, bread and
no one's fed

How Can I Begin to Tell You

Beneath the thick tarp of night
the sea rubs its muscles til the lamps shine
and all the weather drops
massive upon the boards and rocks
How can I begin to tell you
my strangest sorrow grows in what I love
More and more, through the loop of Labrador
and across the narrow Strait
where I made a rough turn in my mother's womb,
past the long bays and islands stolen by causeways,
it's a sound too resonant for speech;
too immense in its clothes to reach a page

Poor, I enter into the warm stations of its blood
into the eternal sea, eternal love,
unstepped paths somewhere above L'Anse Au Clair,
Clarke's Beach and farther, over the elysian geometries
of Conception Harbour and back north
chasin' the lyric ghost across Terrington Basin

And on, tempted on to guitars in cars
and stories wild as the rain stripping the lights
Nights and years we held the other
and spoke bravely of dreams though not aloud
for villages crucified prophets. But held it all
in tongue-tied June,
in our thunder hearts, weeping in the dark
for those cliffs and bays which found us
saying here's your fortune. Sons, daughters;
dogs howling the morning nearer;
baptisms and the yellow light in the funeral house
lived in the woodcuts, balanced and wonderfully-grim,
where all the hills poured their limbs to the harbour

With tons of wind at the window
and a mad fiddle for its voice
how can I begin
My fortune isn't spent and harbours hold the hills
This place drops across my thumb and knuckle
and knows no allegiance to my trouble
and steals my words
and leaves its mark
My strangest sorrow grows in what I love

It Was a Dream

It was a dream. It seemed a month of seeing
where a desert waved, grain by rattling grain
In a soundless place, beneath a sleep
deep where cryptic passages sit and rule
a figure knelt by a cactus
slipped a careful knife into that life
and held his mouth when the liquid dripped

And standing there, turning in a mime
he saw the sun, a brilliant, swinging coin
a trained magnet drawing the sands
drawing the sands to heaven
multiplying hourglasses losing themselves backwards
All tall shifting masses, migrations to heaven
they claimed the high sky. Pouring upward
they were liquid-sand caravans
and he stood upon the bones of the earth

Then it was a dream within a dream. It seemed
a profound town of remembrance emerging
They came with their books and dance
They moved with the careful blood
piling their quilts and nets,
piling their stories and time into the space deserts made
dropped from their shoulders and arms
And they drifted upward, solid chapters where the sands went
Grain by liquid grain they were
soundless caravans surrendering place and time
and sun swung in brilliant tones
and he stood upon the bones of earth

Tongues With Dreams Those Places

Down in the harbour town
old chapters are whipped by words
new language doing their backs. Whips
to split wood those sounds and they split
the old lies like birch with frost

Lies and history are tossed
among the triple-tongued into the barking-pot
a deep-cast lung, a swallowing brew
taking old flags and chains in a slow drag
down, down below time and pain

And let me tell you how we danced:
jig, jig; reel to reel; wall to wall;
a smelter turn of fist and voice;
a throat-burn and arms around stranger and prayer
with a child's wild love and an old one's fear

And When Her Voice Cracks

She wanders and wonders by her Nile
and when her voice cracks
it throws its clothes upon the ground
The lungs labour and are heard
and then laughter, strange laughter
is the last sound
from the thin chest of the bird

A Study From the Hill

I left my room and its slow wheel of quiet
went path and street with the westwind
and stopped to read from a painted rock
where Jeremy and Margaret and love had been;
where Ruth and Rodney crossed their blood
told the world and chalked their name;
where Thomas slept while Raymond sang
though the houses shuddered and the zealots came

Christmas Night, 1993

1

This storm slipped from a prison ship
It leaps through the old city
leaps to gather the breathing and out-of-change
keeps itself a scatter of faces at
windows and locked places
Old as scrolls, wound and ragged,
voice low, voice pitched,
seams shadowed and strange,
it s a range of a life
Will it hide in some crevice or shed
hide its plan til the ship's gone,
the horizon swept clear
and the wake complete upon the land
Or will it whirl here, openly,
furious as foxes in the center of night, bright
with the particulars of festivals

2

This storm's heart is a god
and found, it's a sound of story,
a mass of warm wings
around the tired child where he sings
This night, storm and province slip
from the same prison ship, runic souls
loose and lunging for the flame
that beautiful chaos uncontained
all loose; at full run from
where they were locked in a mute dark

3
Bending through the alleys
with swift legs of dogs,
head-over heels they are the festival gymnasts;
myth-loud, tune by tune
they bring the mood fiddles. And they run
with the carolling bells; they run
with the cognac, nerve by nerve
singing down the frozen throats;
they run with the clocks
nearing new anthems; they spin like cats
then race the corners of this grateful room

They have slipped the prison ships
and run with the fierceness of moons
Aging past the master presence they
leap to their own luminescence

Crosses Upon the Hill

Crosses upon the hills,
brilliant sleeves of light
loved by sons and speakers,
share no bravery, drop no reason
down into the town of stumbled rooms

Past the rusted and strangely-new;
past the raw cathedrals, stoned and glassed-high,
in a harbour small leaps could complete,
turbulence of trawlers make a wake,
a slow braid of gulls and memory

Men, once at altars with the beautiful caution
bred upon nervous and chilling waters,
kneel in strange gardens
holding chaotic the deaf rose

'We can't afford our lives
We can't
afford our lives'
We tremble and fade through wicked treaties
Where is the currency,
remuneration for dreams and visions
for the curing of fears
upon the wind-mad Widow's Walk

Bold cliffs rise like funeral father and mother
folded shoulders above the mute child
Trawlers lean through invisible parentage
to dark places and
mourners sign their hearts from the harbour-sides

Though before the terror of the deaf rose
we are poor and always dying
our tongues have dreams;
our hands have shapes they'll grow
into pots and vessels where light can sail and spin
and beyond the stains crucifying the sight
the sky has tender clouds
for the sun to bleed in and bring
its healing prism

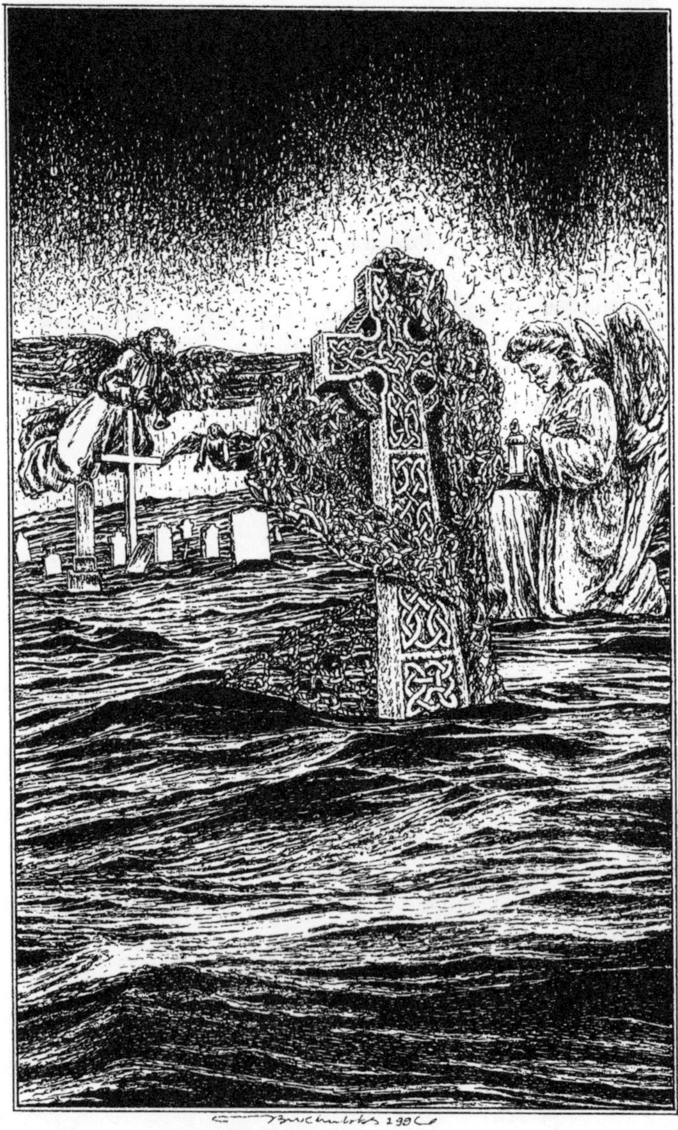

By Churches and Other Fathoms

Turn me a phrase and I'll carry it for you
Any phrase, mother. By churches and other fathoms
I'll make a beautiful komatik. I'll make its runners, berries
and cross-pieces all the mosses falling
from cliffs and damp by the woods. Chaulks will rise
certain with woven reeds thick and golden from the brooks
And how good it will be to see
phrases full and tilting, held to the chaulks
by the barest strands borrowed from last year's webs
And down the long hills
the komatik fastened to the robin's bill
will slip and speed,
no drug to impede its wild ride
And mother, our place will be warmed through
in the long, dense months
when the stoves labour and winter
drops to its knees upon the tribe

Winter Comes

In the yard it lays its clothes
the particular traveller down, around
mummifying tender cedars into
the Madonna and child
Beyond, the southside hills
hum with invisible weight
from this handsome garment,
this ambiguous, long-minded priest
half-enemy; half-saviour

Above, two grey ducks trim
the morning in, call past
to some far, approaching spring

On the awakening avenue
some curse; some sing

The Bells of Winter

Tuned to a clear, deliberate vision
are the bells of winter, a celebrant stirring,
a vintage, something rare in this chase
of snow, wind and time and a brief sun
luring the hiding to race and sing from windows
Chief in their minds, that excessive summer
splitting the rocks and piling possibilities to cliff-tops
and the remarkable figure of clouds and thunder
blessing young limbs tangling in the long wonder
of grass and dream, the green of the warmest dance
that seems always to resurrect and trigger us

And the bells, low across the mummified space,
the softest turn of hips and heads
preserved til rain and warm-lipped winds
spread the covers and cedars leap clear,
bring the other sounds of slower blood and heart
the creeping and keeping close to fires
that shiver and shake when the day folds down
Trading their anthems for memory across the roses
the bells of winter find their time past the hour
And it's all recorded. It's all read and shown
in the known passage of a face; a flower

There's a Dignity
in the Silence Dropping Slow

There's a dignity in the silence dropping slow
A crop of memory brings places
where I can cry peace in the purple furrow by that good plough
and make a shape of air with Durer hands
and lease a lung of time. A soul traces
where I can find doorways and sills my people keep
where they look out through their hymns;
where they sing out where they've been
and form a warm passage through the labyrinth

Sprint from the noise and lies
of parliaments and dark wonderments
Pigeons have seen the full page
have seen it thumbed and turned
and recall it all with a tough push of wings
They sing what they know and never trade their voice,
never twice lay down in another's head

The traveller down the path between my shoulder-blades
picks his time through seasonal and spreading woods
and leans against walls
where young prophets wrote their rhyme
We must know and sing what we're born to
and push through the dug earth—
noise knifing the silence dropping slow

Notes Written by a Gower Street House

And those who leaned close
saw where a fury had stood
by the door, by the thin and tall door
They saw where the fury had stood
and had entered the poor and dying place

Ravens Round the Chimney Pots

There are ravens round the chimney pots
and snow the size of collars
makes the place a tender card
Ghost hills and a windless day
follow the figure where she strays by a stone
and the snow runs to water
where she kneels and sings a ragged tune:
mother, father; mother, father, the looping phase
across windless hills and ghostly day

It's a Glacial Sound That Quiets the House

It's a glacial sound that quiets the house
that locks the doors, boards the windows
And the chimney's an empty yawn
No more will the small feet scatter the stones,
trip the water on spring roads and go
with dream and windflow

This is the land of the eternal caravan
and phantom ox and wagon
fording rivers and straits, hands fierce around
Bibles and other maps. From here to there
is a long-treated road where the whips crack
and the 'huddled masses' stare back

Save a piece of home for our treasure-box
for the worn cedar to breathe. And throw
a prayer to the weather for our long turn of wagons
We are dead many times but twist again
to suck the air in starts and stops
where kettles attempt a song on stranger counter-tops

Lines Written in the Chapel at St. Claire's Mercy

Beloved friend, a quick wind took a leaf
gave me a brief look where it might be
To catch that weathered piece
I'd need to know its place and try to race there
and keep my arms wide
Could the leaf tell
or could only the wind know
where it fell

Water and Time

Water and time slip away
spill their nature, the remainder pulled
somewhere down Nagle's Hill by something,
some wizard's string we can't run and find

I Went to the Harbour Alone

I went to the harbour alone
By the pilots and freighters I thought
this is no place for navigators,
with poor ships and maps
Of all places, this is no oasis

And over the Heights, miserably alone
over the rocks, tough shrub and wind I thought
this is no terrain for travellers
with poor shoes and maps
Of all places, this is no oasis

Back down and over carnival streets, dangerously alone
by the pubs, by doors with guitar drones I thought
this is no place for strangers
with poor hearts and maps
Of all places, this is no oasis

He Said: I am Mad in a Mad Place

A sun is tied to a dancer's waist
and in her leaps and liquid turns
a whole light throws the dance
in replica and splendour across the town
And he said: I am mad in a mad place
Not a trace of the unusual can be found

There are cats and jumpers in a steeple-chase
joined by gulls, bats and dogs
A whole blur of shapes and missions
over and around; over and around
Not a trace of the unusual can be found

A rare mist of roses and lace
lay in loose rows upon house and light
and a child finding the first solid steps,
the first marks upon the fine down
And he said: I am mad in a mad place
Not a trace of the unusual can be found

And love found the lovers, a grace
of fire, comets upon the sky, circling the spires
dropping with time across the water
and fish in thick schools came to the magnet of sound
He said: I am mad in a mad place
and not a trace of madness can be found

Our Stories and Lunging Tongues

Our stories and lunging tongues;
mercury giving words a run;
tuned tendons opening, closing language doors;
scores of lifters arranging the pulse
and looping vowels turning away the false,
breathe motion, fire and choir
into all the inanimates

Memory is a Lantern

In the head it's a luminous sweep
naming whole scapes and shadows
where worlds have buried; have layered deep
In the lungs, the lunging beam,
in its seeking swing and phrase,
distance and history are raised like pillars—
illuminated relief and testimony
raised through the layers to be said,
to be named again, the surge from the recognized
nodding the head, warming the frame
when returning youth and wonder came

For His First Birthday

In the faces of little boys,
through the laughing lights
the carnival wheels of their winded eyes,
stretch the rich fields,
a world, with sense,
might tend and live by

For Tess

My young, treasured and tender friend
I went to the water
and sang a song without beginning or end
with words unknown, unheard, untold
allowing the bold from my mouth and heart
feeling the nouns rub and tumble,
tickle and mumble their happy ways,
parts wheeling and spinning
bucketsful and carts of colour
across the richest, most blinding humble of days

While lying there without thought or age,
a caravan of length; a happy stone,
books of birds and flowers came
and spoke and sang,
spoke and sang your name—
your name alone

Birthday Gift for Brenda

In a corner of this country
upon a road with flowers and other gods
I lifted a stone thrown
from a traveller's shoe
and heard in its roundness
a song for you

December 3, 1994

A world rattles by my window
in its carnival clothes and spin
Here, in the curved home of my straw chair
it's enough and more
to sit and revel and dance and sing
the accomplishments of a friend

After the Storm, a Rare Breeze

1

Dream a little; dance a lot
in or out of your skin
and fit the brief beauty of smooth ponds
into your darkest songs,
lifting gently the night

Trade winds bring
the pure bells of seasons, laying the ringing
across shapes we've made
laying the ringing near the bones of hills
ringing passing down into the breathing bone

Across Henry Street pigeons live
with the remaining bargain of crumbs
and round the laughter of young worlds
they loop like pearls

2

Through my hands
yesterday, churches and old fathoms have slipped
have bent their last knees
on rowdy and rough stones
In the bruised-plum shadows of glass and steel
we chattered and grieved
until the turning chapters of this rare breeze

In this thin layer of loose time
in the music of its good head
through this day, this handsome hybrid,
fallen griefs ease with the kind waters,
the warming flood calling at locked doors and cells

And a fine call through it all can
lead poor souls upon the loved land
to a quieter stretch of home
and silence will thunder til the kind thunder shreds
upon all the berry and lover beds

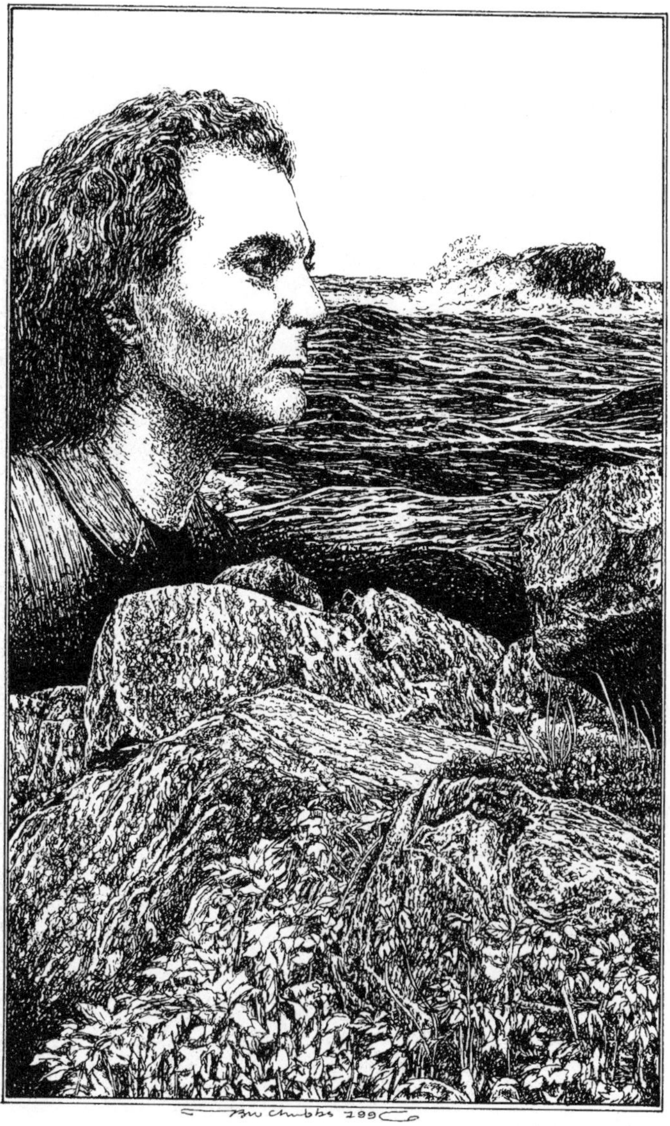

In Cuckhold's Cove

In Cuckhold's Cove strange hybrids grow—
rose and spice; angelica, monkshood, tea;
whole gardens and the long-running sea
and stones and creatures who meet themselves
calling for you and me

There's An Odd Brief of Light

There's an odd brief of light
through the window, across the potter's cup,
up along the ceiling, dropping like fabric
small prints of it upon the marble-black cat
It swindles the ragged tune from my mouth
and puts a song there
How can I fear words breaking,
the love and blood of it shaking apart and passing;
the treaty of language making and unmaking
when a song's in my mouth again
and upon the hill
trees and flowers are deified by a tradewind

Home Thoughts

Boughs blasted and tender; poultices from the juniper;
cool-rhythm brooks through mouths of water;
jigs and spins from reed and wind;
leaping liquid-tongues from the Calvert shore;
trout in fierce speckled-turnings;
and on slow boats to heaven along the Labrador,
within its cobalt basin,
in its lean between islands and sky,
the underside of water is aboil
a bubbled loam spreading again, again to blue
where the passage takes me from words to you

After the Love at Victoria Street

There's a warm hand upon my head
This land and sea have given a hand
to spread upon my head tonight
and I go down to the water to rock and sing
of plentiful and certain things:
the rapid malt of spring and brooks;
trees that shook themselves furious;
curious phantoms upon the rain path;
lain passages of bone and earth;
birth of sundogs and lavender;
fogs more delicate than breath;
sweat from laughter and the spark and fire;
a beautiful liar tender among thieves;
sleeves of light climbing the berry hills;
sills handsome with paint and lace;
a trace of raw sienna in the swimming tickle;
a brace of storms, sermons upon the walking,
talking trees and all around, the fossil barrens,
cairns above home; the purple-grey stone staring;
foam with its clothes, rolling the near shore
and a door thinning where
in a mesh of voice and strings, love goes

I Know Where I Am

When my hands trace the ridge and fold of granite,
that boulder sturdy as god;
when my hand becomes a nation along the lilac stem;
when my eyes follow and measure
geometry of cliffs and water; backs of cats
where they run the sills; race and warp of dancers
where they'll achieve flight and transcendence;
when my ears find gulls and raven
clear and brazen through revved winter;
when I find you, bending from the noise,
the terrible worm through your mind,
the rough lightning striking through the walls
laid low there where you fear, and you rise
with late winter light falling, greeting you
spreading the Renaissance
and peace triumphs and the oceans in your hands
are the heaven tides from the bones in your face,
are the denials against those contriving
their way to some sad, exalted place
and in your speech upon speech, tone upon tone
I know where I am…I am home

September Wedding at Flatrock

1
Memory, whispers and chance
lock a hand over the hearts;
the eaves of a young girl where songs nest
leaving their saying upon that blessed face
I wonder, how can we trace this near thing
and not awaken, bolt to ourselves from dream
Or is it once a breaking day seems
to drop a gift from its hands
and place a path beam through the weather
where we plunge and plunge and drift

2
Above the grotto, above this harbour
where boats once built a cross for a traveller,
straight through the sky,
right with the westwind and sun
the dance has begun
Descended to its home in the feet and head
this baptismal is a myth round the table
up the sleeves of the swinging and wed

I See it From the Paved Hill

I see it from the paved hill
through the changed birch down to the valley
a tally of light and dark in a season rearranged
A figure denies the new prophets
and primes his lantern and books
and edges without chatter by the water and swans
moving with his tracing fire and word
til he's numbered and merged
with the branch and bird

There's no trick or stage
no scheme to enrage the planners, but children
blind from the blinding screens and scanners
point from their windows and wonder at the strange,
the alien trace of time and shadows;
the slow turn through the valley and hours;
and evening lowering
to the ground like a song

Rake the Half-hearted Fire

Rake the half-hearted fire
Condense the ragged blaze
to a yoke of blue, a bare oval,
a shovel of light you or I
could hold and dig with
Take it to a place you know
any place famous with fossils—
furrowed deep with passages
Move the barren with careful love
and hold the whispering sods
Gather the preserved soliloquies and purl
the colours of beauties into patterns,
into the lasting reason of past seasons
as new gospels to live by

Praise

Praise is a paper fire
a loud torch leaping, a flaming rush
raising, pushing the room
then, nothing but a thin sound
an ashen rumour across us
The permanent lights retrace
across the prints, books and face

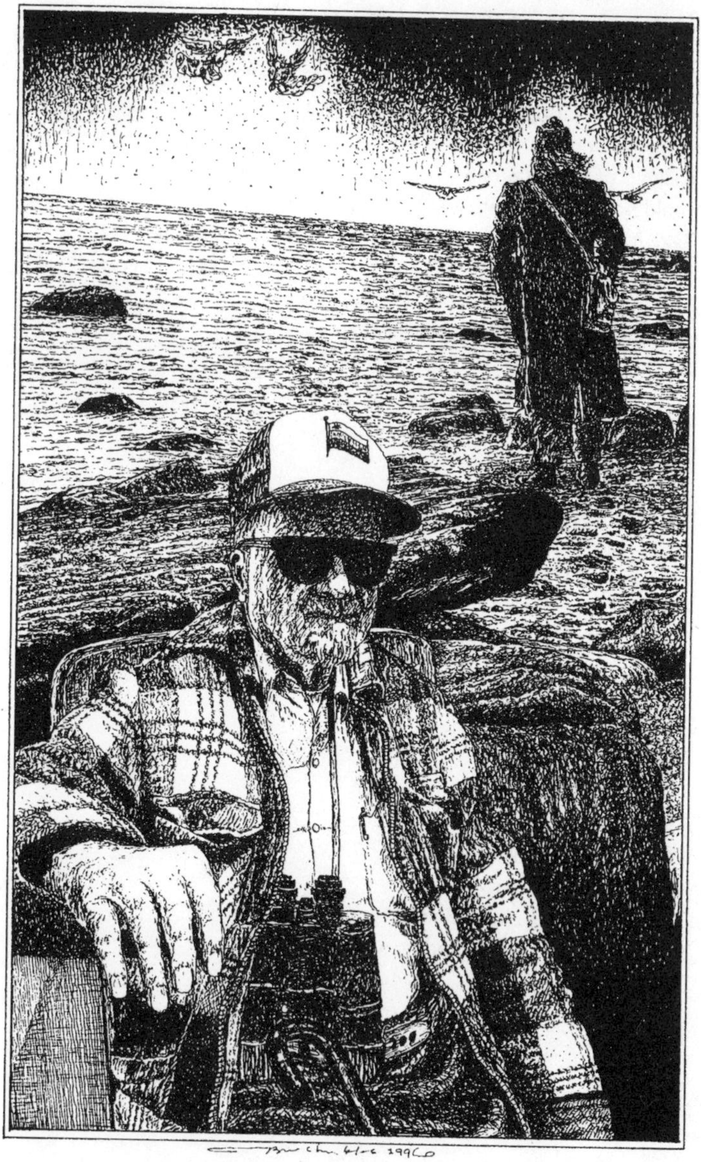

Thundering Houses in the Dropping Light

1
Is it here in the rowdy ruins
we'll find the lost hymns
In this cathedral where I lean
with story-strong O'Driscoll, low
the pure bells call the listeners in
and they come, caps in nervous, beautiful hands;
on their lips the precious kiss and love

2
Summer can bring its own frost
Cry for the mourners, storing themselves on wharves
Rub their rough faces
and a splendid porcelain's found
with a tender filigree all around
The cost of a time is a cruel thing
when beauty is caught in the light drawing away
and through the water, vibrations from an ancient drum
become a rhythm leaving the bay

3
A gull spans the harbour hills
takes the sun for a brief time
laying crisp, rapid shadows upon an old wall
named for lovers and other believers
where young ones with wooden guns fire their names—
small troops marking in play the path to return this way

4
Is it here we'll find the lost hymns
the great-winged sounds, savage voices
though their hearts bled cold
in the black and blue arteries of the soul
It's all a dark mention, here, where a dog's bark
is plenty to collapse a mind
to send a mind past the cliff; beneath the lop

5
We are the sea; we are the kelp
wrapped forever in the brine cologne
Plateaus, sky, steel or guns can't take us from
the wash and rub of the bone
Yes, we are always home

Bury a Bone for Some Later Sweetness

Bury a bone for some later sweetness
Bury it deep beneath secret rocks
by the sea or over the leaning hill
Rows of wind shake toward home
brush the hair of moss with terrible travel talk
and remarkable clouds, pulled to breaking,
sit, mutated thinkers across the ridge

This is the land of all tribes
Dropped here we wrap our feet,
bandage our hands and clear
the black and blue stone. We sit against the purple sky
singing homage though sometimes our hearts split

Deliver us…deliver us from them,
all of them over grim, crucifier distance
measuring us for other burials; other exiles
Can they know our graves are water, rock and air;
caskets, the beautiful waltz and reel;
exiles, the baritone poem
thrown through a vortex, caught and held

Who can sing or measure
our holy, miracle hymns but us—
here, where we bury a bone;
where we cry rough and hold our ragged harbours;
stitch time into connecting rafters
and fill that dancing house full with dancing chapters
Our graves, our burials are here

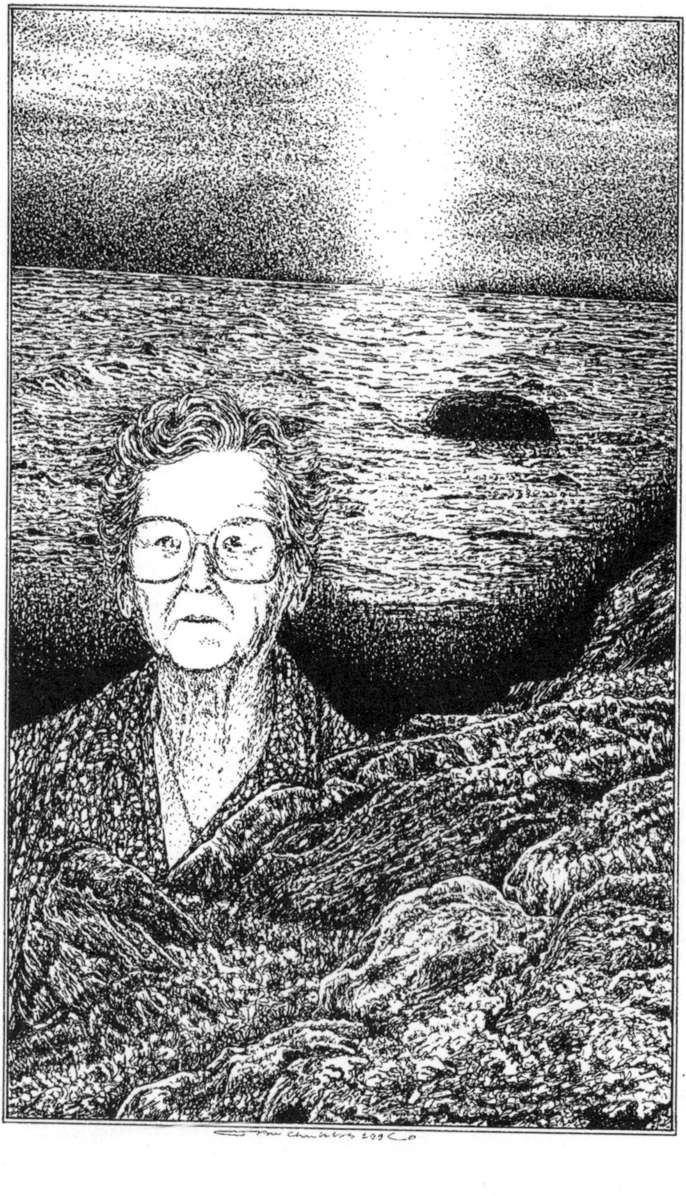

Letter to Maureen

1

You ask how the storms live among us
How do we live among those apparitions
taking our rooms and rumbling
It's a time of myth and muscle, beloved friend
We falter through and kneel,
stay by poorly-made altars and call to children
where they slip to the wild kingdoms

It's a time of myth and muscle
Lovers live in the tough cycle of loss and need
roping themselves to cliffs
Fathers and mothers, more honoured than fiddles,
spread their face against windows
above empty, unholy harbours
Flesh, like storms, riot and rattle
down the long rooms, on the stairs,
a tough rub against chrome and wood
We're never alone
even in our most sacred spots

Out along the road, in a place
carved by light from stone angels,
passing beneath iron-works;
pass the crypts; through the living maze
of perennials and clover,
figures kneel and clear the regions
grown to the sky with bramble and root
In the mute processional, through a sleeve of time
singly they brave the storm drain of light and dark
til with a rough mark of wish and breath
they've crept and fallen upon the stone

2
You ask how we live
among the mosses, bramble and root
Epitaphs and testaments leak through the wonderments
and speak the chorus to everything and no one:
Sometimes it all ends—
the muscle breaks; myths dispel;
heads return to the sweet, clear well
and rooms breathe, clear and true
like proverbs, lichens and lovers do
Because sometimes I sing, sometimes we all sing
blurting a beauty where no storm can win

Dig Through Poor Dreams and Promise

How deep would we dig with thumbs and hunger
to strike the founding head, the first layer
which took with it the first rush
of light and wonder when someone tender
looked and saw this sea and land trace
with rapid blood of fire and shape
and sat with praise upon some peninsula

Dig through poor dreams and promise
through the dark where fancy strangers
pranced down the long-laid carpets;
dig, dig through flags and pageantry,
through colonial waste and bigotry;
dig down through the towns of bones
where the earth still moans its people pass
and on through times never done on pages
of rumour or sound, never said by birds turning
or glaciers and mountains burning

On down to the founding place
that layer, that face with the first light
Dig, dig down straight
learning to ease through granite and pain;
through darkness and the quiet strain of sound
that kept the lamps primed
and held whole races, time beneath time

Dig through the knowing;
dig through the saying
of that layer of the first light,
that layer of sun and the grower's rain
Keep your heart; keep your heart
We are so beautifully-ancient
We are young again

These are the Anthems of Midnight
(In Memoriam, for James)

1

These are the anthems of midnight:
down the long hallways
clocks rubbing their minutes together
bell tones grown, warm stones
rolling the long passageways;
a crack of light from a granite vein
where the moon lifted over and nicked the spot
Oftime this is the delighted flower—
mumbles from prayers or sleeptalk;
slippers of sleepwalk and the looping, crooning yard dogs
round this young and old hour
illuminated shadows, the ivy heart purpled and caught

2

By a room where the maples pray
a spare crow crosses and rattles
and a pale hand reaches for bakeapples—
sun rises in a bowl of light

3

From all things read, all things silent and said;
from all benedictions dropping slow
between winds and other religions
comes the full beauty of sound
Campbell, Goudie, Squires and Wade found
And this is the tangle of our way
these anthems we circle and place down

And You, Blessed Healer

1

Let me pray my own way—
steeples in my workroom;
towers of love and time above me
where I lift a warm chalice to everyone

I kneel here not for the distant poor,
weeping forms in some imagined passageway
I kneel for Trinity, the Bight and Cartwright;
Ship Cove, Nain and Black Duck;
Burin, Fogo and Lodge Bay

2

Bring buckets of fire
Cauterize the raw sounds and light whole towns
where lamps have gone down
Voices, voices rise with the earth and sea
Tales and tides wash across
liquid bandages for the raw,
large talk of immortality, the fierce-age forever
It's not enough against the rough breath, the dark cough
eyes melting into long hallways
Enough for an evening
for touching the flesh, arms around the spare frames
and whole places where they're leaving

3

Snow holds the stains
until the rains take them, bend
seasons to hide the day, draining the tough evidence,
the earth opening and closing
losing the wounds and cries living made
We turn from the ribbed sounds
sliding the blinds down—sip tea and memory

4
A wind blew a healing in
a warm turn of air through his October heart
beneath the icon and Bach
releasing the morphine trick, and slipped him
beyond nations and stations;
beyond the text bringing his body round
for the last draft of crows, maples, hills and town

5
The dying hates the living; the living, the dying
Pathways of light across barrens and other rooms
are lost compass points when the heart drops cold
when crevices that can't be jumped
lean wider, away from the reaching
Oh and how it warps the loving
Can't see the waves or the water
Can't hear the thunder though it baritones farther
and farther still
warm light leaks upon the harbour and sill
but the heart has dropped cold
and the giving and taking dropped with it
for the dying and living
crave the other's soul

6
But the hearts of the beauties
the hearts of the beauties know
past the edge of belief lies the freedom
Yes, faces in a lilac tree;
a tender mass on a singing Eve;
a way to breathe when the sky is stolen;
daughters bringing mirrors to swollen rivers;
the last round, repeating sounds
bells for the spirits going home

Paths to prosperity go through the soul
lightning moves detours and shadows
speaks through woods once too dense for travel
We own the space we stand in,
sleep, breathe and dance in
pronounce it ours and sing its name
Freedom is a lamp upon the word
is its own universe
and planets growing wings from their bones
know they aren't thrown to century heaps
and stars sensing chill where the fire turns low
blaze in their passage and know they'll be praised

Yes, past the edge of belief lies the freedom
and through the stumbled pathways
we bandage the grief
and mark its grave with beautiful stones

7

Have you seen the knots the sea can tie
a puzzle held in one hand;
a language so strange
I can only nod and never attempt its name
Its speaks there for all to hear
on wharves and across this rocked, mossed land

I've heard mad men, genius with the rope
fade and cry at the solid twist
of trawl and jigline so strange
they could only nod at its name
and drop the tough trade from their wrists

And I've seen the sainted, our province-mothers,
the builders and saviours, in the jaw of storms
go to the shore in fierceness,
but they could only turn and cry
at the knots the sea could tie

And I've seen you, blessed healer, resurrect the flesh and sound
where we swept the rooms with prayer
and laid our hearts down
And you nodded there for us to hear
untying the knots the sea had made
calling each by its name—undoing for us, its strange trade

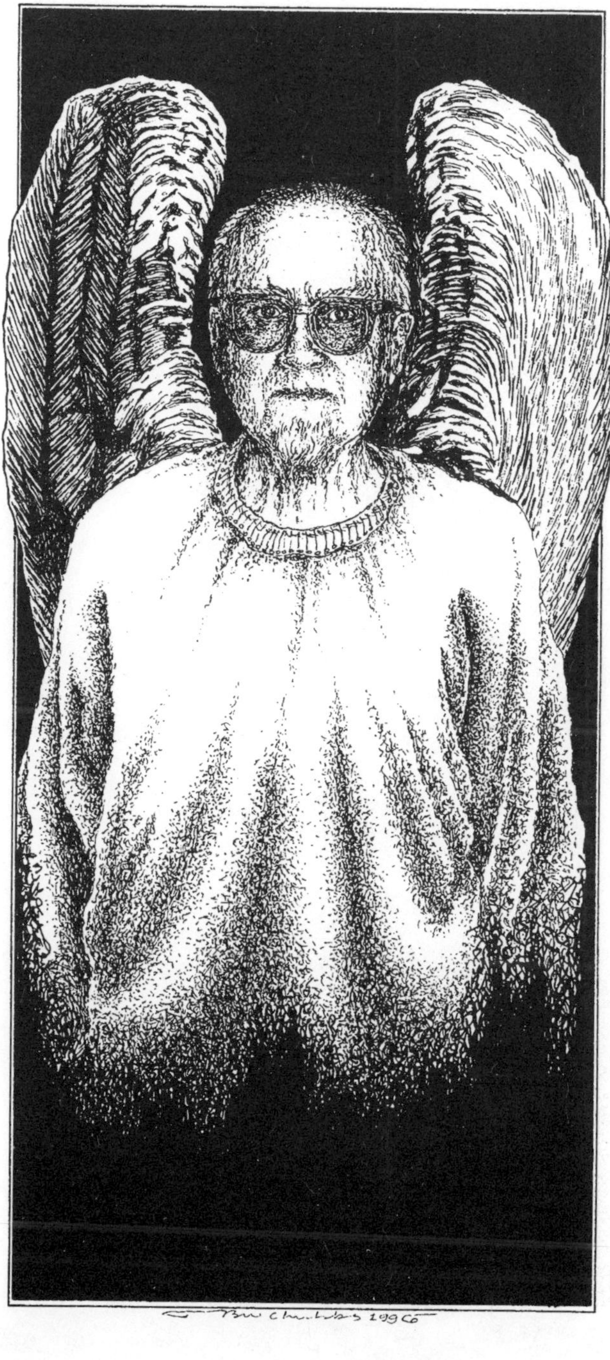